D0115545

Also by Eileen M. Berry

Roses On Baker Street

HAIKU
on your shoe

by Eileen M. Berry

Illustrated by Dana Regan

JOURNEY
FORTH™

Greenville, South Carolina

Library of Congress Cataloging-in-Publication Data

Berry, Eileen M., date.

Haiku on your shoe / by Eileen Berry ; illustrated by Dana Regan.

p. cm.

Summary: Jeremy's mother encourages him to make friends with a new student from Japan who is learning English.

ISBN 1-59166-374-1 (perfect bound pbk. : alk. paper)

[1. Friendship—Fiction. 2. Japanese—United States—Fiction. 3. Schools—Fiction.] I. Regan, Dana, ill. II. Title.

PZ7.B46168Hai 2004

[Fic]—dc22

2004024868

Designed by Craig Oesterling

Illustrations by Dana Regan

Composition by Melissa Matos

© 2005 BJU Press

Greenville, SC 29614

ISBN 1-59166-374-1

15 14 13 12 11 10 9 8 7 6 5 4 3 2 1

To Daddy,
who has always nurtured
my love for storymaking.

Contents

Chapter 1

On the day of the first snow, a new boy came to our school. He walked into our classroom with tiny snowflakes in his black hair. *Like stars,* I thought.

He sat down in an empty desk and did not look at anyone. Scott, the boy beside me, whispered, "Bet he can't speak English." His name in Japanese was something long and hard to say. But it started with *Taka.* Miss Eastman said we could call him that for short.

1

Scott pretended to eat an invisible taco. I glanced at Taka, but he only stared straight ahead. The snow in his hair had melted. No more stars.

Miss Eastman stretched up tall and pulled a map down from above the board. She pointed to a green landmass. It seemed to float in the blue water on the map. "Here is Japan," she said. "See the water on every side of it? What do we call this kind of landmass?"

Lily's hand was the first to go up. "Oh, oh, oh!" she gasped, as if she were taking her last breaths. Sometimes I thought she must know everything. "An island," she said.

"The island of Japan is Taka's home," said Miss Eastman.

I looked at Taka again. Now he was staring down at his desktop. *What would it be like to have an island for a home?* I wondered. To me, islands had always seemed like scary places. Lonely places. Water on every side. All you could see for miles. I wondered if Taka liked living on an island.

When we had English, Taka went off to a special class.

"Told ya," said Scott. "He doesn't speak English."

I wished I didn't either. Miss Eastman made us underline pronouns. I wondered what Taka was doing in his class.

Chapter 2

After school, there was just time for a snowball fight before the bus left. All the boys joined in. Except Taka. He watched from the edge of the playground.

It was perfect snow for making snowballs. I rolled four or five at a time and stuffed them in my jacket pockets. It's a good plan, but you have to throw them fast. Otherwise you have pockets full of soupy slush.

I had thrown my last two snowballs at Scott and was stooping down to make more. I was only a few paces from Taka.

All of a sudden—*plop!* A snowball hit Taka in the head.

Everything grew quiet behind me. The game had come to a complete stop. All the boys were watching Taka.

I was standing closest to him. "You okay?" I asked.

Taka looked up. Then down. Then sideways. We waited.

Scott let out a high, ringing laugh.

Slowly Taka raised his hand and wiped snow from his forehead. "Okay," he said. His chin went down inside his coat. He walked away.

The air felt colder then. I didn't feel much like playing anymore. I was glad when it was time to get on the bus.

Mom met me at my bus stop. As our boots crunched homeward, I told her about Taka. I told her about the snowball. I told her about Scott's laugh.

Mom's gray eyes matched the sky, that gray look that it has before a snowfall. "Taka could use a friend, Jeremy," she said. "Why don't you invite him over?"

I shifted my backpack. "I might," I said.

I thought about it all the next day. I thought about it when I saw Taka sitting by himself on the bus. I thought about it when I saw him standing on the sidelines of our football game at recess. I thought about it when he returned from his special English class and put his head down on his desk.

But I never did it.

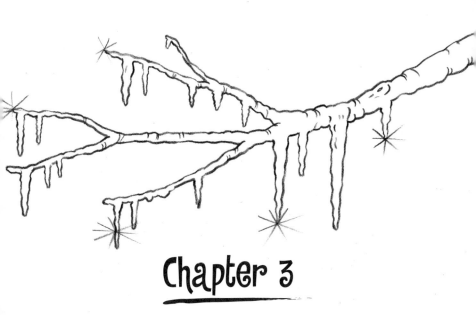

Chapter 3

During the night rain fell and froze on cars and trees and fences. Mom and I walked down to the corner to wait for the bus the next morning.

"I thought about it, Mom," I said. "But it's too hard to talk to Taka. It's like talking to . . . an ice cube."

Wind rattled icy branches. I shivered.

"Jeremy," Mom said, "imagine how it would feel to be in his shoes. He's come halfway around the world to a place where everything familiar is gone."

I stared at my boots. Mom wrapped her arms close about herself and bounced on her tiptoes.

"Some people are like these trees," she said. "All closed up in ice cases. At least, it seems so sometimes."

I gazed around.

She reached to break a long, skinny icicle from an oak branch. She held it between her thumb and finger. "It's hard to reach inside—beneath ice." She handed me the icicle. "But God wants us to try. And ice melts, Jeremy. With God's love, it does." Her gray eyes looked into mine.

I nodded.

She winked at me and pulled my cap down over my ears.

Chapter 4

That day in English class we read poems

about winter. Miss Eastman said they were

haiku, the kind of poems people write in

Japan.

"Lily, would you please read the first poem

on the page?" asked Miss Eastman.

Lily loved to read out loud. She cleared her throat and raised her book so she could look over the top of it as she read.

Full moon in clear sky
looks down into a mirror
of new fallen snow

Lily closed her eyes and lowered her book. Scott snickered.

"Do you understand?" Miss Eastman asked. "The poet thinks that the moon and the snow look very much alike. To him they look as much alike as a woman and her reflection in a mirror. How is the moon like snow?" Her gaze roved through the room. "Scott?"

"Um." Scott's face turned very serious. He stared at his book for almost a full minute. "They're both white?"

"Oh, oh!" Lily gasped. She waved her hand around in the air and wiggled her fingers.

"Lily?"

"They both have a beautiful glow."

Miss Eastman smiled. "You are both right," she said. "What a group of poets I have today!"

Scott glanced over at me with a smug face.

All of the poems were like that. They all had three lines. None of them rhymed. I didn't understand them. I wondered if Taka knew about this kind of poem.

5 _____

7 _____

5 _____

Chapter 5

"For Friday," Miss Eastman said, "I'd like each of you to write a haiku about winter."

I sighed. I wasn't good at poems.

Miss Eastman wrote the numbers *5, 7, 5* in a little column on the board. "A haiku has this many syllables in each line."

"What's a syllable?" asked Scott. He forgot to raise his hand.

Lily's hand shot up. "Oh, oh! I know! A part of a word," she said.

"Sometimes it's a part, and sometimes it's a whole word by itself," said Miss Eastman. "It just means a beat."

I looked out the window. What did syllables have to do with Japan . . . or poems . . . or winter? The sun was out. I watched an icicle just above the window dripping as it slowly melted. *Drip . . . drip . . . drip.*

Suddenly everyone around me was clapping, slowly and rhythmically. I snapped back to attention. We were reading the moon haiku again and clapping on every beat. Every *syllable*, I mean. It was kind of fun.

Rachel, who was always quiet, raised her hand. "Miss Eastman, these poems are so small," she said. "Why do people want to write such short poems?"

Because they want to get it over fast, I thought.

Miss Eastman smiled. "Let me ask you a question, Rachel," she said. "Do you like only big things? Like skyscrapers and oceans and elephants? Or do you like small things too? Like snowflakes and ladybugs and dimes?"

Rachel smiled back. "I like both. Sometimes I like small things better."

"A small, quiet poem can have much more meaning than a long, noisy one," said Miss Eastman. "Small things can be just as important as big things. Sometimes even more important."

あ

Chapter 6

I sat by Taka on the bus that afternoon. He was reading. I glanced sideways at the book. Funny, scrawly symbols filled the pages. No letters.

"Taka," I said finally. "We live pretty close to you. Do you want to come over? We could go sledding." I held my breath.

He stared at me for a moment. "Hmm," he said. He looked up. He looked down. He looked out the window.

I swallowed to keep a long sigh from coming out of my mouth.

"I think . . . no," said Taka. He smiled shyly. Then he opened his book again.

I let out the long sigh. After that I stayed silent.

"I tried this time, Mom," I said later in our kitchen. Mom had lit the candle on the table. We were eating gingersnaps and drinking hot chocolate. "I really tried."

"Yes, Jeremy, you did. I'm proud of you."

"But I didn't get anywhere."

Mom dipped her cookie into her steaming mug. Then she looked right at me. "How do you know?"

"He said no. He didn't want to play at my house."

Mom took a bite and munched slowly, savoring. "It may seem like nothing happened. But something did."

"What?"

"You took a small step in the right direction."

I watched the flame of the candle. Around the wick a pool of clear, melted wax was forming. A tiny drop of wax rolled over the edge of the candle and dripped down the side. *Small things can be just as important as big things,* Miss Eastman had said. *Sometimes even more important.*

Chapter 7

That night I worked on my haiku. I tried to write about icicles, about snowmen, about hockey players. But I ended up with only a pile of crumpled paper.

Thursday morning on the school bus, Scott and I sat behind Lily and Rachel. Lily turned around in her seat. She whipped out a sheet of notebook paper and raised it like a flag. "Would you like to hear my haiku?" she asked.

My mouth dropped open. "You're already done?"

Lily sat up very straight and tall. "See what you think of it."

She cleared her throat.

> *Ice maidens skating*
> *like beautiful winter swans*
> *on ice-covered lakes*

"What in the world is an *ice maiden*?" asked Scott.

Lily frowned at him. "An ice maiden is a beautiful young lady."

Scott looked at me. "Have you ever seen one?" he asked.

I shook my head. "I've never seen swans skating either," I said. "How can the ice maiden skate like a swan if swans don't skate?"

"How can she skate at all if she's made of ice?" asked Scott. "Maybe she should be playing freeze tag instead."

Lily rolled her eyes. "Forget it," she said. She turned around in her seat. Her chin tilted up a bit.

Scott grinned at me and held out his hand for a low five. I didn't give him one.

I leaned forward. "I think it's a small step in the right direction," I said.

Lily smiled, but only halfway.

Rachel had been very quiet, thinking. "Maybe it would be better if we wrote about *real* things," she said. "Things that we've all seen before."

"Like snowball fights!" said Scott.

"Like watching snow fall—from inside, by a fireplace," said Rachel.

"Like . . . like . . ." My voice trailed off. I still couldn't think of anything.

Chapter 8

We had art class that day. Our art teacher, Mr. Crocker, always wore bright ties and a big smile.

"Have you all heard that it's supposed to snow tonight?" he asked us. "The weatherman said four to six inches."

We all cheered. All except Taka. He just sat quietly.

"In honor of the snow," said Mr. Crocker, "I thought we'd make snowflake mobiles."

Mr. Crocker handed out white paper. Soon we were all folding it into triangles and making tiny cuts with our scissors. Mr. Crocker put on a recording of music that had sleigh bells in it. He whistled while he walked around the room.

Mr. Crocker stopped by Taka's desk. I looked over at Taka. He already had three snowflakes finished, and now he was folding a new piece of paper.

Mr. Crocker's whistle changed to one long, low note. "Wow!" he said. "You're doing a super job. What's that you're making now?"

Taka looked up at Mr. Crocker. He looked down. He glanced around. He finally held up the paper figure without answering. It was a little bird, shaped from the folded paper.

"Class, it looks like we have an expert in the Japanese art form *origami,*" said Mr. Crocker with his big smile. "That means making shapes out of folded paper."

We all looked on in wonder. Taka's eyes flitted sideways. He didn't seem to know who to look at, so he studied his desktop again.

Mr. Crocker set the little bird back down. "Someday soon we'll have a lesson on *origami*," he said. "Maybe Taka could bring in some other designs to show us."

I thought I saw Taka smile—just barely— as Mr. Crocker moved on.

Chapter 9

I had already decided what to do when the end-of-school bell rang. I dashed to Taka's desk before he could stand up.

"Taka," I said. "That bird you made is cool."

Taka picked up the bird and looked at it. Then he looked at me. I wasn't sure he understood. "I mean, it's great!" I said. He smiled.

"Do you know a lot about paper folding?" I asked. "Do you do other animals?"

He looked down at his hands. "Umm. Little bit."

"Do you think you could teach me?" I asked.

He looked up. "Teach?"

"Yeah! I'd like to learn. Maybe you could come to my house after school. You could show me how to fold paper and make stuff."

He stood up quickly. "I not come today," he said. "I have homework. English." He smiled shyly. Then he turned and headed for the coat rack.

Back at my desk, I grabbed my snowflake mobile and stuffed it into my backpack. The paper snowflakes got crumpled, but I didn't care.

34

Chapter 10

Mom poured me a second cup of hot chocolate that afternoon. "The weather forecast says snow tonight," she said.

I didn't say anything. I didn't even smile. I could feel her watching me.

"What's wrong, Jeremy?" She plunked three marshmallows into my mug.

I stirred the marshmallows around and around with my spoon. "Do I have to keep trying?" I asked. "Every time I invite Taka over, he says no. I don't really want to do this anymore."

"Hmmm." Mom's sigh faded away, and she said nothing for a while.

I kept stirring. The room was so quiet I could hear the clock ticking. Slowly my marshmallows turned to shapeless blobs.

"Some things take longer to melt than ice," said Mom finally. "Marshmallows, for instance."

I looked up. "I wouldn't want ice cubes in hot chocolate."

"No?" Mom smiled. "You wouldn't have to wait as long to see them disappear."

I thought about that.

"Sometimes we wait and wait for things to happen. For people to change. Don't we?" said Mom.

Now I knew what she was talking about.

"We feel like giving up on them. It's too hard to go on showing love. That's what we think sometimes. Right?"

I nodded. I stared into my mug and tried to drown one of the white blobs with my spoon.

"But what if God thought that way about us?"

I stopped trying to drown the blob. I sat very still.

"Imagine if God said, 'I'm tired of loving Jeremy. He doesn't always treat Me right. Haven't I shown him enough kindness? I'm giving up.'"

"He wouldn't," I said.

"And neither should we."

Mom leaned over and looked into my mug. The marshmallow blobs had turned into a white froth. We smiled at each other.

Chapter 11

A beam of light slanted through my room early the next morning. It lit up the crumpled snowflake mobile dangling over my bed. Mom's head poked in. "No school today, Jeremy. Sleep later if you want."

I threw off the covers. "More snow!"

I sprinted across the chilly floor and flung back the curtain. Sure enough. The bushes were big spotted lumps. The fence posts wore powdery caps. And the trees had vanilla icing on every branch.

After breakfast I bundled up in my coat and cap. I pulled on the boots with fur inside. As I was tugging on my mittens, the phone rang. I heard Mom say, "Let me ask Jeremy."

Mom stepped up beside me. "It's Taka's mom. Would you like to go to his house to play in the snow?"

I stopped with my hand halfway into my mitten. Slowly my eyes met Mom's. Hers were sparkling. "Today?" I asked.

She put the phone to her ear. "We'll be there in ten minutes," she said. "I look forward to meeting you." She put down the phone and smiled at me.

I stared at Mom. "Taka's mom speaks English?"

"Beautifully." She pulled my cap lower over my ears.

Chapter 12

I cleared my throat as we knocked on Taka's door. My insides felt kind of cold. My heart pounded.

Taka opened the door. "Come in," he said with a shy grin.

We stepped inside. A tidy row of shoes stood beside the door. Big ones for Taka's dad, medium-sized ones for his mom, and small ones for him.

Taka's mom had a shy grin like Taka's. "So glad you come today!" she said. Her voice was soft . . . like a snowflake's landing.

Mom was taking her shoes off. I looked down uncertainly at my furry boots.

"Jeremy," said Taka's mom. "Taka . . . he really want to play with you. But he feel a little scared to go where everyone speak English. He want me to invite you here."

Imagine how it would feel to be in his shoes, Mom had said. I eyed that small pair of shoes by the door. And suddenly, I understood.

Taka pointed to the table. "Origami," he said.

"Wow!" I moved closer to the table. Spread out on the red cloth were dozens of little paper figures. I picked up a dog, and then a pig, and then a sailboat. Some of them looked very hard to make. "These are great!"

"Cool," said Taka. "Later, I teach. But first . . . we play in snow?"

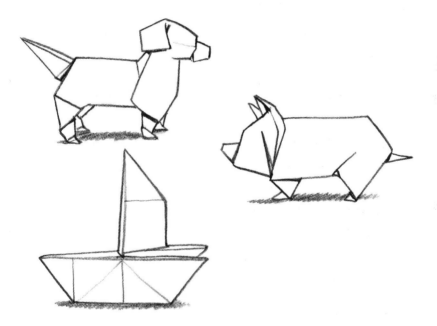

It was the best snow day I ever had. Taka and I built a snowman. I learned to say *snow* in Japanese. And I learned that ice melts. Much faster than I thought.

Chapter 13

"Go inside now?" Taka asked.

We heard laughter in the house. Warm air swirled around us when the door opened. I remembered to take off my boots as soon as I stepped in.

Mom and Taka's mom were sitting on the black couch. Behind them on the wall were two big fans painted with bright birds and flowers.

My mom was trying to say something in Japanese. And both grown up ladies were giggling like the girls in my class. I looked at Taka. He clapped his hand to his mouth and began to shake with silent laughter. I had never seen him laugh before! I laughed too.

"What is my mom saying?"

Taka looked at me and then at my mom. He listened to his mom.

"She say, *Ohayo.* Good . . . morning."

I looked at him. "Ohio, Taka," I said.

He waved his hand. "Good morning."

Sitting at Taka's table, I drank my first-ever cup of hot tea. Through the steam, my eyes settled on one of Taka's small shoes by the door. That's when it came to me. My first-ever haiku.

"Do you have some paper?" I asked Taka.

I scribbled out my poem on a scrap of his origami paper.

It happened so fast that I was sure the syllables were wrong. But I clapped the rhythm softly. It was right! I read it again. It was *real.*

Chapter 14

Taka leaned over to see my paper.

I laid down the pencil. "I wrote a haiku on your shoe," I said.

Taka looked up. Then he looked down. Then he looked over at our moms. He walked to the door and picked up one of his shoes. He frowned and turned it over and over. Then he picked up the other shoe.

"What are you doing?" I finally asked.

"You wrote . . . haiku on my shoe?" he said. His eyes were dark and puzzled.

I thought very hard for a moment. Then I smiled—but I didn't laugh. "Not *on* your shoe, for real," I said. "I wrote a haiku on your *shoe*. I mean, *about* your shoe."

Taka's chin went down inside the collar of his shirt. "English," he said. "I not get it."

"That's what I thought too," I said. "About haiku, I mean." I looked down at the three short lines on my paper. "You'll get English, Taka. I'll help you." And I really wanted to. Maybe something inside me had melted too.

Taka looked right at me. Not up. Not down. Not sideways. His eyes shone when he smiled. *Like stars,* I thought.

Haiku for Taka

My boot and your shoe
in snow puddles at your door
just like two good friends

Make a snowflake

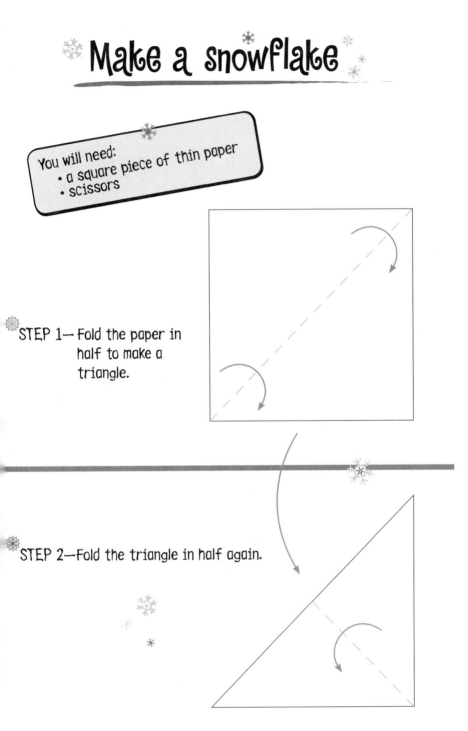

STEP 1— Fold the paper in half to make a triangle.

STEP 2—Fold the triangle in half again.

❄ STEP 3—Fold it in half again, OR... ...fold it in thirds.

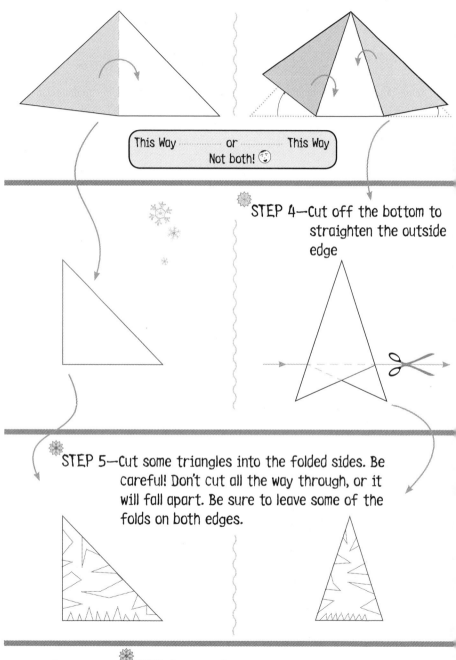

This Way ······ or ······ This Way
Not both! 😊

❄ STEP 4—Cut off the bottom to straighten the outside edge

❄ STEP 5—Cut some triangles into the folded sides. Be careful! Don't cut all the way through, or it will fall apart. Be sure to leave some of the folds on both edges.

❄ STEP 6—Unfold your snowflake.

Fold an Origami Bird

You will need:
 • a square piece of thin
   paper

Look at each picture and hold your paper just the way
it's shown. The dotted lines are the folds. The arrows
show which way to fold it.

STEP 1—Fold along the dotted
line, crease it, then
unfold.

STEP 2—Fold the lower edges to
the center crease with-
out overlapping. Crease
the new folds.

STEP 3—Turn the diamond shape
over and fold the lower
edges to the center
crease without overlap-
ping. Crease the new folds.

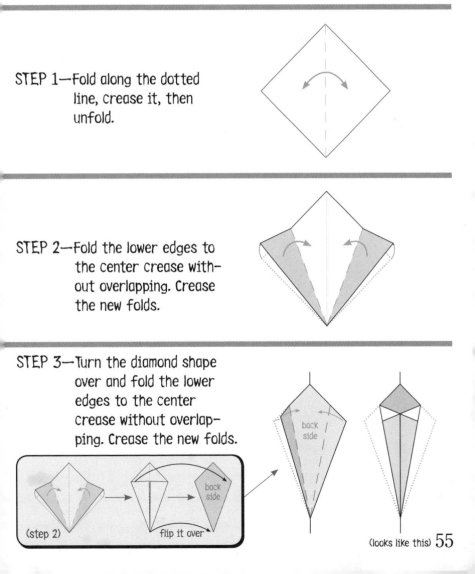

(step 2)

flip it over

back side

back side

back side

STEP 4—Fold the bottom point up
almost even with the top
point. This will become
the bird's neck.

(looks like this)

STEP 5—Fold the front tip
down to make the head.

(looks like this)

STEP 6—Fold the bird in half, keep-
ing the head on the front
side and folding the wings
toward the back.

STEP 7—Pull the neck forward
and crease the paper at
the bottom of the neck.

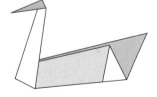

Taka's bird was harder to fold than this one. You can
find other origami patterns in books at the library.